First published in 1992 by
Cornerhouse Publications
70 Oxford Street
Manchester, M1 5NH
061 228 7621

© Mike McCartney
The right of Mike McCartney
to be identified as author has been asserted
by him in accordance with the Copyright,
Designs and Patents Act 1988.

ISBN 0948797 17 7

Design and Production by Wordsmith, Manchester
Printed by Jackson Wilson

Published in association with National Museums & Galleries on Merseyside
to coincide with the exhibition Mike McCartney's Merseyside at Merseyside Maritime Museum.

NATIONAL MUSEUMS & GALLERIES
· ON MERSEYSIDE ·

mike mccartney's merseyside

introduced by willy russell

Cornerhouse Publications in association with
National Museums & Galleries on Merseyside

To Rowena and the brats, my family and the people of Liverpool and Merseyside

With thanks to:

Richard Foster (Director), Lorraine Knowles and N.M.G.M.; Black and White printer Terry Cryer (Leeds 6); Colour printer Colin (and Philip) 'L. T. Colour Labs'; Willy Russell (and Mums); Howard Mortimer and Wirral Borough Council; Graham Souness, Chris Moss and Liverpool F.C.; Carl Hollins and 'Talia'; Vivienne Tyler and E. Chambre Hardman House; Tony Hirst and Ellesmere Port Boat Museum; Martin Harrison and Mersey Travel; Keith Naylor and Cammell Lairds; Joanne Wood and Atlantic Tower boss; Rod Gadd and Cathy, Royal Insurance; Philip Alcock and Liver Building; Captain Mucklow and David of the Navy; Joan Gadd and the Merseyside Tourist Board; Eric Leatherbarrow and the Mersey Docks and Harbour Company; Mike, Lee and Dave 'Click'; Mandy and Mike 'Colourcraft'; Diana Day and M.D.C.; John Gillard and Mersey Tunnels; Mitch and plane and to everybody else who helped me with my Merseyside shoot "Thank U Very Much".

Mike McCartney was my favourite photographer even before I knew of his existence. Back in the times that my kids now refer to as 'the olden days', the fifties and sixties, when Liverpool was the centre of the universe, I used to buy the best music paper in the world - Merseybeat. In other, national music papers, the pictures of the musicians, the groups and the solo singers were okay ... but they weren't *real*. Even when the Shadows or The Vipers or The Whoever were supposed to have been caught by the lens in a casual, offstage or behind-the-scenes manner, there was still a posed, self conscious and ultimately 'removed' quality in the pictures. The same was true of the onstage pictures; visual images, intended to convey the rude and threatening joy of rock and roll managed instead to convey merely the *fact* of an event having taken place, whilst the *truth* of the moment remained uncaptured, unrecorded. Between the pages of Merseybeat however, were pictures which had at their heart a truth as recognisable as that of the music. Many of these pictures of then local bands in a local rag were taken by Mike McCartney who acted as unofficial official photographer to his brother's band. Even if these bands had remained local, had not gone on to become world famous, these would still have been great pictures and a testament to a photographer who can recognise and capture fleeting moments which life itself seems to have momentarily stage managed.

I suspect Mike McCartney has always known that when presented with a great subject, the photographer should just shoot, and not get in the way. In Merseyside, Mike has just such a great subject, and being a native he understands the eloquence of the region and its people and in these pictures, allows Merseyside to speak or, perhaps, sing for itself. This is not a collection of didactic pictures, not a civic or commercial attempt to 'sell' Merseyside as a beautiful place. Yet, I suspect that any number of them would be seized on with glee by a PR person charged with the job of promoting the area's image; for what Mike McCartney celebrates is the beauty that *is* here, be it in the Irish face of the woman on the ferry, the kids on Everton Heights, looking at the rooftops that seem to stretch almost to Wales or in the clouds above the Mersey - a picture which for me immediately evoked Django Reinhardt playing 'Nuages'.

Mike does not balk at shooting the more 'obvious' Merseyside icons and images. When he does so, however, he makes us look afresh, or from a new perspective, at things so familiar - especially to those of us who live here - that we almost take them for granted. I'd never realised what an ominous and threatening thing that Liver Bird could be, until I saw it shot from below, its clenched beak jutting out like some malevolent alligator snout. The river Mersey is perhaps one of the most photographed waterways in the world. For that reason alone, other photographers might have shied away from the subject, choosing instead to find a more esoteric or determinedly alternative feature of Liverpool. Mike however, knows that like a Monroe or a Garbo, the River is a true star,

one which just cannot be ignored and whose secrets will never be fully captured by the lens, no matter how many millions of feet of film are devoted to it. And so he goes for it head on, capturing in colour its capriciousness along with its massive power and splendour or, in black and white, evoking (with the help of the QEII) memories of the forties and the fifties when this was a working river and every time you looked you saw those big seagoing monsters bound for the Africas or the Americas.

Last year I had the pleasure of seeing Mike McCartney, the photographer at work. One had to look hard and long to recognise that he was actually 'at work'. Photographing a group of clamouring, excited kids in a packed theatre bar, Mike merely became one of them, using his tiny camera almost as a plaything. There was never a moment in which the photographer and his process became more important than his subject. These kids trusted him, were at ease and unselfconscious with this photographer in their midst.

From the pictures collected here, it seems that Mike McCartney had exactly the same effect on Merseyside.

Willy Russell
Liverpool
May 1992

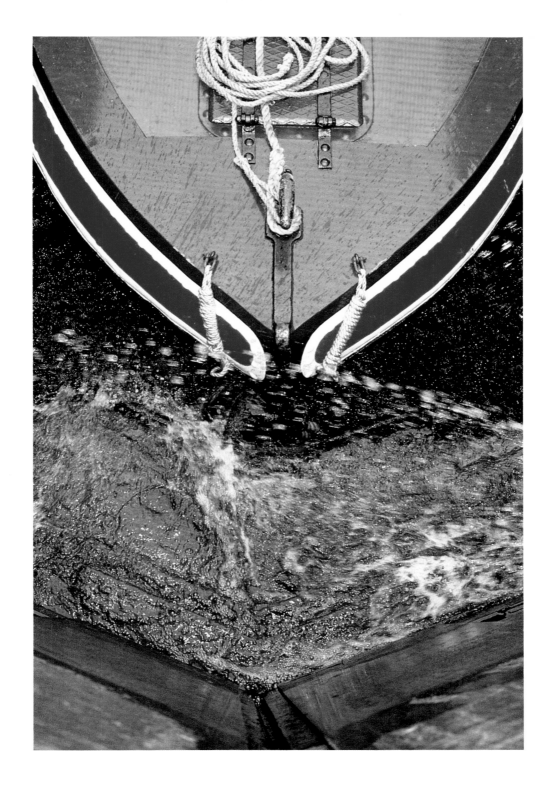

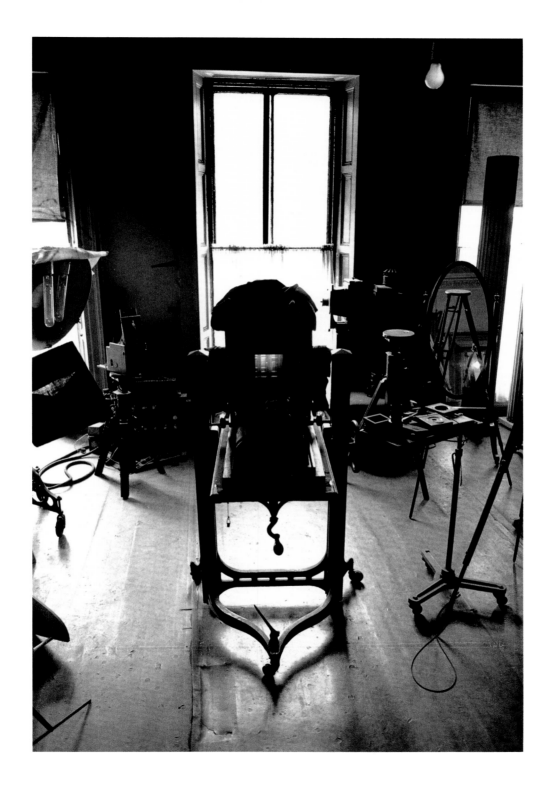

9. Cloud over Liverpool
   Taken on an unusually sunny day for 1991 this image is my tribute to photographer E. Chambre Hardman, Dublin born 'master of clouds'.

10. Vent Shaft Shadow on the Mersey
    Having put my camera away as I'd finished shooting Liverpool from my lofty perch on top of the Mersey Tunnel Vent Shaft, I had to get it out again when God suddenly put on his light to cast this giant vent shaft shadow on to the River Mersey.

11. Liverpool Skyline
    Taken from the top of the Queensway Tunnel Vent Shaft, this bright strip of City between grey sky and river includes the Liverpool Post and Echo building, the Royal Insurance, Atlantic Towers and Everton Heights, the Pierhead, the Law Courts and Beacon, the Albert and Catholic Cathedral, Wapping Dock and Anglican Cathedral ... to name but one.

12. Inverted Liver 1
    A mirage image of one of the Liver buildings reflected in a puddle 'down the Pier'ead'.

13. Inverted Liver 2
    Taken from the top of the Royal Insurance (the tallest building in Liverpool?) the Liver shadow, reflected in concrete.

14. Car Mirror 1
    The Royal Liver Building with a half-renovated Waterloo Warehouse sinking into my Sierra rear view mirror.

15. A Reflective Liverpool
    When surrealism offers itself freely (in this case a distorted image of our famous Liver taken through the window and bonnet of my car) ... I never turn it down.

16. Liver Bird Ready for Take Off
    The Liverpool Flying School emblem proudly displayed on the tail of Mitch's plane at the old Speke Airport, where years earlier as kids, we'd watched the 'Bird Man' plummet silently to his death when his parachute failed to open!

17. The Boat and the Bird
    Taken from the roof of the Atlantic Tower Hotel, the golden boat at the top of St Nicholas's church (where cousins John and Jane Mohin got married) upstages the rather better known Liver Birdy.

18. QEII - Framed
    The magnificent Cunard Liner, on a visit to Liverpool in 1990, dwarfing even the Albert Docks!

19. Liverpool Lady
    About to depart the ferry at the Pierhead, this lady with the strong Liverpool-Irish face (which could tell a thousand and one stories) reminds me of my aunties, grannies, and great Grandparents ... all wrapped up in one.

20. Liver Lines
    Taken from Riverside 'Priory Wharf', Birkenhead, between Woodside and Cammell Lairds.

21. The Shadows at the Albert Dock
    Shortly after the opening of the Albert, an unusually quiet shot of the waterfront (it now gets six million visitors a year!).

22. Two Way Look
    By a girl and her dog on New Brighton Beach, opposite Vale Park, with Polly and Becky about to jump in the Mersey!

23. Royal Liver Sails
    It's twenty five past Liver Clock, through the sails of Carl Hollins's yacht TALIA during the Mersey River Festival 1991.

24. Three Planes and a Yacht
    Taken from Carl Hollins's TALIA, three Toyota display biplanes leave their vapour trails over the TRAJAN during the Grand Parade of Ships to mark the end of the River Festival '91.

25. Tall Ship Blasts Ferry Across the Mersey
    Just after boarding the famous Mersey MOUNTWOOD and plundering all her booty, the ZEBU'S canon finish off the job.

26. Tall Ship at Sunset
    At the end of a summers day the OCEAN YOUTH CLUB comes to rest in the calm waters of Albert Dock.

27. Tall Ship on the Mersey 1991
    Looking for a serious sea battle (as part of the Grand Parade of Ships, to end the River Festival, June 30th) the ZEBU even upstages the Liver Buildings, Pierhead *and* the Albert Dock!

29. This *is* Anfield
The sight (to send shivers down the back) which greets every visiting team to Liverpool F.C. ... *just* prior to stepping on the hallowed turf!

30. Michelle and the Lads
After thirteen painful operations on her legs, young Michelle Pratt's courage gets her onto the Anfield pitch as Liverpool's mascot, escorted by John Barnsey, Gary (now Evertonian) Abblett, and Stevie Nicol. Bruce Grobbelaar, the best goal keeper since Bert Trautman, is in the distance.

31. Liverpool Lad with Hanky
Sharing a private moment with the 95 Hillsborough dead. One of the cards read 'In loving memory. Love and miss you Lee. Mum, Joe, Andrew and Joanne XXX'.

32. In Loving Memory
The card resting next to Gary's beloved Liverpool FC scarf reads 'We miss you so much ... The pain still goes on. We also remember the other 94'.

33. 95 Red Roses
It's now *THREE* years since the tragedy at Sheffield. 95 living roses, laid at Liverpool Cathedral 2.45, April 15th 1991 to remind the world not to let it happen again.

35. Long Boat at Lock Gate
Good job I've got six kids! To get this shot I had to stand on the top of the Ellesmere Port Boat Museum Lockgate as it was opening, and nearly did the splits!

36. The Ellesmere Port Ghost Boats
Four narrow boats at rest in the Ellesmere Port Boat Museums still waters - upside down!

37. The Big Red Jug
One of the many beautifully painted objects to be found aboard many of the Ellesmere Port Boat Museum's Noah barges (also check the door and hatchway paintings).

38. GONC RVIC
A self portrait at Ellesmere Port Boat Museum, or as Stanley Unwin would say 'a self porthole taken in the portrait of a barge'.

39. Sub Through Rusty Laird Lockgate
As I'd just been to the launch of the first Hovercraft across the Mersey, I was in my best suit, but desperately wanted this shot through these rusty 'portholes'of perhaps the last submarine, UNICORN, built on Merseyside. To enable me to get the shot (by lying flat out across the wide dock gate in my posh clothes) Mike the security man lent me *his* coat to lie on.

40. War and Peace
Possibly the final two subs to be built on Merseyside at Cammell Lairds, overlooked by Merseyside's oldest building (circa 11th century) ... the Birkenhead Priory.

41. Rio or Rock Ferry
This chamois leather handed gent, plus amazing costume is actually walking the streets of Liverpool 8 (just before it rained!) as part of the wonderful 'Caribbean Carnival', which parades through the city in August each year.

42. Street Party I
As it is carnival time again, permission is given to seal off Wendell Street, hang up the bunting and balloons and get the good old trestle tables out.

43. Street Party II
Danny's ever-open door. In the old days, Liverpool doors were open *all* the time for anyone to drop in. Sadly these days (as in most cities) the front door only usually stays open at party time.

44. Street Party III
The 'main man' of Wendell Street Party ... Danny and friend prepare the hanging of the balloons.

45. Self Portrait Through Joe's Eyes
Taken in Wendell Street, Liverpool 8 just prior to the street party celebrating Merseyside's International Caribbean Carnival.

46. The Palm House
Taken in its hey day (before the yobs broke all the glass panes and it had to be boarded up) this *was* the Palm House in Sefton Park. Hopefully, when those actually responsible for this elegant example of Victorian architecture see this photograph, it will remind them to set about restoring it to its former glory (with a moat of Pyrhana fish to keep it that way?).

47. Exclusive! Rarest Flower Grows on Merseyside
It could only happen up here ... one of Britain's rarest species, the Snake Head Fritillary, grows like a weed every year on our garden path!

48. Max and his Monster
Young man feeding his pet Stegasaurus (tentatively!) in the grounds of 'Gullivers World' on the outskirts of Liverpool (where he keeps the beast).

49. Dusty Slide in Vale Park
Fun with Aunty Dorothy round the front of the band-stand with their 'Joy Time' talent contest (which gave you Keith Chegwin, Sonia, ... etc) but the *real* fun round the back!

50. **Wedding I - The Bride and Groom**
When the veil of Jan, the bride, blew away at this Merseyside Wedding, it revealed the loving attention of 'Dracula' Groom, Paul.

51. **Wedding II - The Two Photographers**
'This way' suggests main cameraman Mitch to the Bridegroom and Bestman (posed between Ian (Ex-Echo) McCulloch and Henry (Christians) Priestman) but Royal, hand-behind-the-back, popposer Hambi, pips him to the post.

52. **Lights, Camera ... Action!**
Taken in the portrait Studio of E. Chambre Hardman in Rodney Street with just *some* of the props used back in the forties and fifties.

53. **Rodney Street Through E. Chambre's Camera**
The studio of the late E. Chambre Hardman, Rodney Street, Liverpool, with just *some* of the cameras therein. Hopefully one day, not only the studio, but also the whole house, will become a world famous museum, as a tribute to the great man.

54. **Eye Eye**
Two eyes trying to outstare each other in Tate Gallery darkness, during a video art exhibition.

55. **John Moore's 17**
At the seventeenth John Moore's Liverpool Exhibition at the Walker Art Gallery, and in front of Albert Irvin's bright Belfast 'Skipper' canvas, this triangle of art lovers (plus baby) is topped by two mothers-in-law , Willy Russell's and mine, deep in acrylic debate.

56. **Silence of the Lambs**
On the way home from Chester my wife Rowena spotted this board sign in the middle of a field filled with 'Quality Welsh Lambs', happily munching the grass! (It's enough to turn you veggi.)

57. **George Harrison - Pin Up**
A surreal song lyric leaflet lying in the gutter outside the Bluecoat Chambers. I *hope* the pins are acupuncture!

58. **Bo on ... Drums!**
Exclusive shot of early blues influence, guitar great, Bo Diddley, not on his more famous oblong guitar, but on *drums* at Peckforton Castle, near Chester.

59. **Bo on Guitar**
Bo Diddley live on stage at Peckforton Castle with his famous oblong 'Turbo - 5 speed' ('Brang It To Jerome') guitar, narrowly avoiding two lightning bolts of scaffolding.

60. **George and Albert**
Who else in that outfit but George Melly, Liverpudlian, Art critic, Jazz singer and friend, exiting stage left at the Albert Docks 'Wharf' to rapturous applause (but not from John Chiltern and his Feet Warmers ... they want him back, to sing the encore!).

61. **Don't Shoot, I Give In**
Taken at the Paul McCartney Kings Dock Concert, 1990, tell me whose hands are up in the spotlight, and I'll give you the answer when we meet.

62. **C Moon I**
Not in fact a shot of 'Colditz' prisoner of war camp, but actually the Liverpool King's Dock Paul McCartney Concert audience, taken through the gauze of a giant screen.

63. **C Moon II**
Ex-Average White Band classy lead singer Hamish Stuart breaking off for a second from the early evening Kings Dock Live performance to welcome the photographer ... 'Oivay, already so soon the noo Michael'.

64. **And all because the lady loves ... fireworks**
A Milk Tray, chocolate box sky holds two 'Pretty Flamingo' fireworks over the waterfront at the June 7th display to mark the opening of the Eleventh Mersey River Festival 1991.

65. **Tina Turner Firework Over Liverpool**
Everything was going fine when I started shooting the River Festival Fireworks with 'Photographer's assistant' Nigel, but half way through, panic set in when *both* of my cameras started to fail me. After my Rollei Magic had completely jammed and the 'B' setting on my Nikon 'F' started playing up (with the most beautiful fireworks going up in smoke before my very eyes) I finally settled for a one second Nikon exposure and at least I got this deep black for Tina's haircut to explode into.

67. **Rainbow Over the Pool of Life**
Taken from Woodside Ferry (thanks to Ronny Fogg) the end of this rainbow landed in Melbourne, Australia.

69. **Young View Over Liverpool**
The original Norse name of Liverpool was Hlither Pollr - The Pool of the Slopes. This young couple are getting the best views of the city and the distant Welsh hills from Everton Heights, where my Dad and his family were brought up.